People of the Bible

The Bible through stories and pictures

Jesus and John the Baptist

Copyright © in this format Belitha Press Ltd, 1985

Text copyright © Catherine Storr 1985

Illustrations copyright © Chris Molan 1985

Art Director: Treld Bicknell

First published in the United States of America 1985
by Raintree Publishers Inc.
330 East Kilbourn Avenue, Milwaukee, Wisconsin 53202
in association with Belitha Press Ltd, London.

Conceived, designed and produced by Belitha Press Ltd,
2 Beresford Terrace, London N5 2DH

ISBN 0-8172-2037-2 (U.S.A.)

Library of Congress Cataloging in Publication Data

Storr, Catherine.
    Jesus and John the Baptist.

    (People of the Bible)
    Summary: Retells the story of John the Baptist,
who prepared the way for Jesus, and recounts the
early teachings of Jesus.
    1. John, the Baptist, Saint—Juvenile literature.
2. Bible. N.T.—Biography—Juvenile literature.
3. Jesus Christ—Baptism—Juvenile literature.
4. Jesus Christ—Teachings—Juvenile literature.
[1. John the Baptist, Saint. 2. Jesus Christ—
Baptism. 3. Jesus Christ—Teachings. 4. Bible
stories—N.T.] I. Title. II. Series.
BS2456.S79   1985   232.9′4 [B]   85-12281

ISBN 0-8172-2037-2

First published in Great Britain in hardback 1985
by Franklin Watts Ltd,
12a Golden Square, London W1R 4BA

Printed in Hong Kong
by South China Printing Co.

  23456789   89 88 87 86

Jesus and John the Baptist

Retold by Catherine Storr
Pictures by Chris Molan

Raintree Childrens Books
Milwaukee • Toronto • Melbourne • London
Belitha Press Limited • London

In the days of Herod the King, there lived in Judea a Hebrew priest called Zacharias.

One day, Zacharias was in the temple when an angel appeared and said, "Your wife, Elisabeth, is going to have a son. You must call him John. He will be a great teacher."

Zacharias said, "How can I believe this?
I am an old man, and my wife is old, too."
The angel said, "Because you have not
believed me, you shall be dumb until what
I have told you comes true."

Soon after this, Elisabeth found that she was going to have a baby. Her cousin Mary came to visit her. Elisabeth said to her, "You are blessed among women, for you are going to be the mother of the Lord. You should call your baby Jesus."

When Elisabeth's baby was born, she was
very joyful. Her neighbors said, "Let us
call the boy Zacharias."

But Elisabeth said, "No, he shall be
called John."

Zacharias made signs that he wanted to write. When he had been brought a writing tablet, he wrote, "His name is John." Then he found that he was no longer dumb, but could speak again.

John grew up and became a preacher. He went to live in the wilderness, eating locusts and wild honey. Many people came to hear him. He told them that they should repent. And he baptized them when they confessed their sins.

The people asked him, "What shall we do?"

John said, "If a man has two coats, he should give one to a man who has none."

Then they asked him, "Are you the Christ?"

John said, "No. Someone will come after me, whose shoestring I am not worthy to untie. I baptize you with water, but he will baptize you with the fire of the Holy Spirit."

12

Soon, Jesus came to the River Jordan to be baptized by John. John said to him, "Why do you come to me? I should ask you to baptize me."

But Jesus said, "No, it is for you to baptize me."

When John did this, the Spirit of God came down from heaven like a dove, and God's voice was heard, saying, "This is my beloved Son, in whom I am well pleased."

Jesus went up into the wilderness and fasted. After forty days he was very hungry. The devil tempted him and said, "If you are really the Son of God, turn these stones into bread."

Jesus said, "It is written that man needs more than bread; he needs the word of God."

The devil took him to the pinnacle of the temple in Jerusalem and said, "If you are really the Son of God, you can throw yourself down from here. God will send his angels to keep you safe."

Jesus said, "It is written, 'You shall not tempt the Lord your God.'"

Then the devil took Jesus up a very high mountain and showed him all the kingdoms of the earth. The devil said, "If you will fall down and worship me, I will give them all to you."

Jesus said, "Get thee behind me, Satan. It is written that we should worship none but God."

Then the devil left him, and Jesus went back to Galilee.

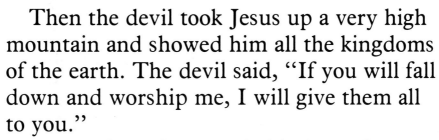

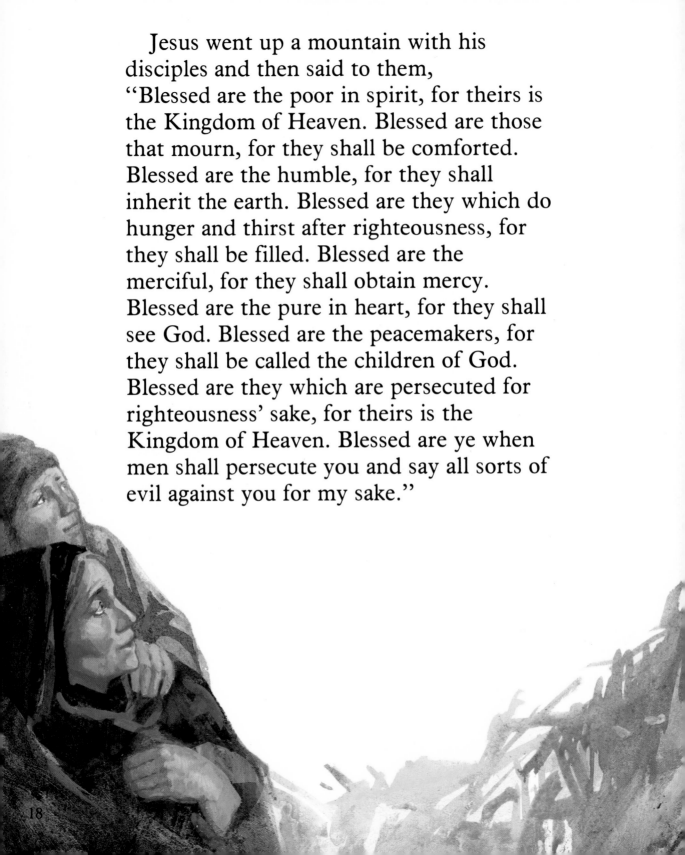

Jesus went up a mountain with his disciples and then said to them, "Blessed are the poor in spirit, for theirs is the Kingdom of Heaven. Blessed are those that mourn, for they shall be comforted. Blessed are the humble, for they shall inherit the earth. Blessed are they which do hunger and thirst after righteousness, for they shall be filled. Blessed are the merciful, for they shall obtain mercy. Blessed are the pure in heart, for they shall see God. Blessed are the peacemakers, for they shall be called the children of God. Blessed are they which are persecuted for righteousness' sake, for theirs is the Kingdom of Heaven. Blessed are ye when men shall persecute you and say all sorts of evil against you for my sake."

Jesus said, "In the old days, we learned to claim an eye for an eye and a tooth for a tooth. But I tell you that if a man hits you on the right cheek, you should turn the other cheek toward him. You have been told to love your neighbor. I tell you to love your enemy. Don't be anxious about your lives. Look at the birds. They don't work, God feeds them, and you are far more important to him. Don't trouble yourselves about what to wear. Look how beautiful the lilies of the field are. They do not toil, neither do they spin. But Solomon in all his glory was not as beautiful as they are."

21

One day the disciples asked Jesus, "Who is the greatest in the Kingdom of Heaven?"

Jesus called a child to him and said, "I will tell you, unless you become as simple as a child, you will never enter the Kingdom of Heaven. You must be humble and ready to learn, like a child. Anyone who is kind to a child, is being kind to me. But if anyone is unkind to a child, it would be better for him to have a millstone hung around his neck and to be drowned in the depths of the sea."

Everyone in Judea talked about Jesus and his healings and teachings. Now the disciples of John the Baptist came to John and told him of these things. John sent two of his disciples to Jesus to ask, "Are you the one we have been waiting for? Or should we wait for another to come?"

Jesus said to them, "Go back and tell John what you have seen here. Tell him that the blind can see and that lame people are walking. Tell him that lepers are cured, and the dead have come alive again, and that the poor people listen to my teaching."

25

Now Herod the King
sent his soldiers to bring
John to put him into prison.

Herod had married
Herodias, who was the wife
of his brother Philip. John
had told Herod that this
was wicked. When Herodias
knew what John had said,
she was furious and longed
for his death, but she did
not know how to bring this
about.

On Herod's birthday there was a great
feast in the palace. Salome, the daughter of
Herodias, danced in front of Herod.

Her dancing pleased him so much that he said, "You can ask me for anything you like, even if it is half of my kingdom. I promise to give it to you."

Salome went to her mother and said, "What shall I ask Herod to give me?"

Herodias said, "Ask for the head of John the Baptist."

So Salome said to Herod, "Give me the head of John the Baptist."

When he heard this, Herod was afraid of what people would do if he put John to death. But he had sworn to give Salome anything she asked for.

He sent an executioner to kill John, and his head was brought to Salome. John's disciples took his body and buried it.

When Jesus heard of John's death, he knew that quite soon he must go to Jerusalem where he, too, would die.

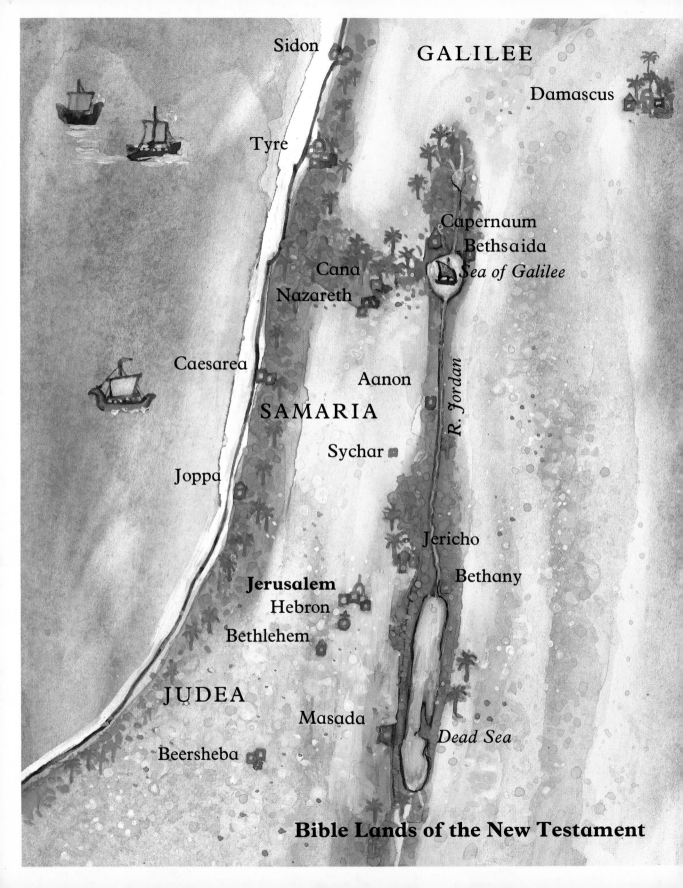

Bible Lands of the New Testament